FOR THE ANIMALS
WHO MISSED THE ARK

Jim Barton

Plain View Press
P. O. 42255
Austin, TX 78704

plainviewpress.net
sb@plainviewpress.net
1-512-441-2452

Copyright Jim Barton 2008. All rights reserved.
ISBN: 978-0-911051-39-1
Library of Congress Number: 2008937649

Cover and title page photographs by Cathy Barton.

Acknowledgements

My humble thanks to the editors of the following journals and magazines who first published these poems: "At the Bird Museum" in *The Aurorean*; "After the Rain," "Buffaloes," "The Fishwife's Tale," "Hurricane," "October, Country," "Only a Boy," "Queen of Kings," "Sense of Place and Order," "Toy Soldiers," "Two Hawks," "Wake-up," and "White Wedding" in *Between the Lines*; "The Old McLemore Place" in *Contemporary Rhyme*; "The Noah Gene" in *Cotyledon*; "Postscript to the Epistle to the Animals Who Missed the Ark" in *Foliate Oak, Best of Foliate Oak*; "Muscadines" in *Ibbetson St. Press*; "Blackberries" in *Parnassus Literary Journal*; "Faith of my father" in *Perspectives*; "End of Summer" in *Poesia*; "Life on the Surface" in *Raw Dog Press*; "Today" in *Red Owl*; "Coastal Warfare" in *Sea Stories*; and "Respect," "Instructions for the Design of a Kimono," "Home," and "Hawk, Snake" in *Snowy Egret*.

Contents

    Acknowledgements   2
    Epistle to the Animals Who Missed the Ark   7

Part One: Storm Clouds   9

    June   11
    Muscadines   12
    Blackberries   13
    Little Prairie   14
    Home   15
    Respect   17
    Riding Fence   18
    Two Hawks   19
    Hawk, Snake   20
    Queen of Kings   21
    Late July   22
    Borders   23
    Hurricane   24
    End of Summer   26
    Warclouds   27
    The Noah Gene   28

Part Two: The Rains Begin   29

    Life on the Surface   31
    History of a Cloud   32
    Shooting Star   33
    Daughter   34
    White Wedding   35
    Bird   36
    Only a Boy   37
    Diamonds, Rubies   39
    The Old McLemore Place   40
    Sense of Place and Order   41
    The Beaver   43
    Instructions for the Design of a Kimono   44
    The Fishwife's Tale   45

Part Three: Deluge — 47

Life Oak — 49
Wash & Dry — 51
Still Waters — 52
Blue Boy — 53
Final Fling — 54
Crossing Over — 56
Wake-up — 57
Faith of My Father — 59
Buffaloes — 60
Vespers — 62
At the Bird Museum — 63
The Theory of Devolution — 64

Part Four: Rainbow — 65

After the Storm — 67
Coastal Warfare — 68
After the Rain — 69
Today — 70
Advice — 71
Outsiders — 72
Roots — 73
Song — 74
October, Country — 76
Crow's Feet — 77
Toy Soldiers, Hardwood Floor, Bag of Marbles... — 79

Epilogue — 81

Postscript to the Epistle to the Animals ... — 83

About the Author — 85

Dedicated to:

*Marie Barton, Viola Barton, Cathy Barton,
Glynn Calahan, Marzell Smith and Dana Washington*

*For all their support, encouragement,
beauty and wisdom*

Epistle to the Animals Who Missed the Ark

Oh, if only there had
been room in the in-
side, warm and dry
safe from destruction
safe from fear...
we're still here of course
struggling day by day
adrift on unfamiliar seas
seeking answers
wondering
if we even know
the questions
treading waters
we've imagined for ourselves
desperately clutching
clinging to first one object
then another vainly
straining to keep our heads
above it all
for as long as we can
before sinking
slowly sinking
into the oblivion
that even now rises
around us
soft animal eyes
flickering their welcome
from its depths
   the echo of distant splashes
   the hollow wails of the doomed...

Part One: STORM CLOUDS

June

Clouds,
like summer children,
          stretch out
on a field of blue,
stay
all afternoon.

Muscadines

These are God's vineyards;
He sowed these wild grapes Himself,
draping them as garlands
from the tree-crowns,
tendrils trailing
like lovers' fingers
hovering above a thirsting earth.

Here, in the late sun
and smothering dust of August,
I prop my ladder
against the pines,
an aluminum stairway to Heaven's
prizes, hanging heavy.

Below, where they've overwhelmed
the bushes, they are almost
wholly ghost-like,
dusted in the wake
of four-wheeler saints
and pick-up pilgrims
out for a Sunday ride.

But, up here,
in the canopy,
where squirrels fly and birds
take rest from flying,
the fruit hangs plump and dark, and
the pungent musk
sends me soaring
over the vaunted vineyards of men:
    the sun-kissed hills of California,
    the lush, looping valleys of France,
    the stairstep terraces of Italy,
and it is enough for me
to see, to touch, to taste, to know
that here, in my little piece
of the sun-parched South
grow God's grapes—
and they are very good.

Blackberries

Sweet summerkisses
whose lipstick stains
the soul, lingering ghostlike—
half taste, half memory,
through barren months, until
in Spring, juices flow anew,
and love-songs sweep
from field and fencerow,
through thorny thicket
gathering dark clouds
of migrant butterflies,
blue pilgrims, winged
worshippers, keepers
of a flame that blazes black,
life's sweet blood, sweet memory,
sweet summerkisses.

Little Prairie

Now is the time I love it most,
this city-lot slice of wild prairie
between my back fence and the neighbor's yard.
Grasshopper sentries, ever-vigilant,
ride the strawgrass tops,
stalks rustling stiffly in the breeze;
thick stands of bahia cling
to rich, dark soil with pale ghost fingers,
remembering a past whispered
long before men came
to tame, to carve, to shape and to plow.
Here, wildflowers paint ever-changing canvasses
worthy of golden frames—
shocks of pink and purple,
shouts of sharp yellow,
sighs of angel wing white.

Above, lazy cloud-wagons skirt
the bright blue plains,
passengers peering through the flaps
pointing and laughing, waving
at this little island of hometown prairie
in the heart of a sculpted green sea.

Inhaling the fresh scent of freedom,
I tip my straw hat with a smile.

Home

The huge hickory had snapped
about twenty feet up,
jagged bone-splintered trunk
standing still in mute shock,
the great top now resting
on limbs and elbows
in this muddy hollow off the power line.
I'd been cutting it for firewood,
my saw growling, all grit and grab,
chips and spent dust spewing,
as chunk after chunk hit the ground,
dull thuds on the leaf-mash.

We'd filled the back of the pick-up
'til it rode pregnant and low with its load;
one last piece remained behind,
and I trudged back down to retrieve it.
I bent and saw the elephant-skin bark
had peeled back, and there in the light,
a family of beetles was busy:
   the shock of relocation,
   the crushing death of a few,
   panicked flight for others,
   the cold, hard truth settling in,
still, this loyal remnant stood fast.

Grabbing both ends of the section,
I shook my head in wonder at
the stay-at-home determination
of these orphans whose future
I held in my hands.
Perhaps it was in the knowledge
that they'd come from a broken home:
I could no more think they're just insects
and brush them away with a glove
than the liver could reject the kidney
or the heart could refuse the hands.

Continued

Gently I nudged what remained of their home
to a quiet, protected cove, turned and climbed the hill.
Happiness, for some, can be summed up
as simply being left alone.

Respect

Returning to my truck by a different path,
eyes on the ground before me,
I nearly run into it face-first.
How long it had taken her to spin it
I can't say—
half an hour? Half the morning?
Most of the day?
I could destroy it in seconds
with a swipe of my machete,
wipe it out with my body
clumsily tramping up the trail
bucket in hand
loaded with lighter pine
chipped from an old sappy stump.

I'm sure the afternoon glare
glinting off my glasses
must have given her pause
wondering what sort of strange creature
was this, with eyes to rival the sun.
The dappling of light
bouncing off her silken web
certainly stopped me dead,
where now I stand
on the edge of a whispered question,
her future in the flick of my hand.

Smiling,
I tip my cap,
leave the trail
and wind among the trees
'til I've passed,
leaving her to a well-deserved rest
head-high
in her own
little place
in the sun.

Riding Fence

Leftover barbed wire loop
hangs on weathered post—
   the spider has woven
her
own
dream-catcher.

Two Hawks

He knifes the air
with crisp cuts headfirst
in a hook-and-claw dive
then instantly pulls
up and up
with practiced ease—
flash of red, glint of cream
underbelly-gleam
like the moon.
She swoops and soars
twirling currents
only she and he
can feel.
Midair they dance
alone together,
world spinning
furious
below them,
silent save for the whisper
of windrush
through their perfect,
matching feathers.

Hawk, Snake

The ancient scarred oak leaned slightly
marking the home-bend in the road,
not so much encroaching as permitting
the path and its travelers to pass.
Approaching on foot in the thick evening air,
I spotted a red-tailed hawk,
unruffled and perched on an out-thrust limb,
intent on her target below.
Transfixed, I stood 'til she cocked her head,
launched herself with two easy beats,
and sailed to the nearby pines.
There, shoulders hunched,
head thrust low, she glowered.

Resuming my walk, I rounded the bend,
and there in the dust of the tire-ruts
lay a healthy young moccasin coiled
and frozen at the thrum of my footsteps,
flattening and fattening his body,
tail twitching silent in warning,
the cottony shroud of his mouth agape.
Grabbing a stick, I picked him up
and eased him to the side of the road,
then glancing back once as a caution,
I left this place
where being somebody means nothing,
where being is all that there is,
and whistled my way toward home.

Now, in my swing, I breathe easy.
Though the hawk has flown elsewhere for supper,
and the snake's just a shadow in deadfall,
a near-silent "s" in the leaves,
I smile as I soak up the evening—
> I can still feel the gnarl of oak in my talons,
> taste the bite of the dust on my tongue.

Queen of Kings

It was all so perfectly innocent:
(a boy, a bucket, a snake),
a perfect end to a summer day—
grinning his way back home,
his pride and his find both
barely contained as he
summoned us out to the porch,
in the twilight out on the porch.

A kingsnake flecked with spots of gold,
(constrictor and hunter and friend),
its tail, cut short by someone's blade,
now rounded and on the mend.
A young adult, it appeared to be,
healthy and three feet long—
we studied it there on the lawn,
by the sycamore, out on the lawn.

He watered and caught the kingsnake food,
(crickets and lizards and skinks);
he made it a home in his snake-box,
a nest with grasses and twigs.
He sheltered it from the sun,
protected it from the rain,
in its hideout under the porch,
in the darkness under the porch.

Two weeks passed by in silence,
(the snake, the bucket, the boy),
when the tale began to twist.
There, in the box with the kingsnake,
six perfect ovals lay
glistening white on the nest.
We gathered around the box,
in silence around the box.

And our mouths formed perfect ovals,
our eyes opened wide with joy,
at the box and the eggs and the wonder
of the bucket, the snake, and the boy.

Late July

The little creek is nearly dry,
and all along its crusted banks
the thirsting trees are curling
tendriled toes for just a touch
of the precious, trickling water.
See how they raise their crusted arms
to Heaven and cry for rain;
how at night their papery leaf-cells scrape
dry rasps in the slightest breeze;
how when morning comes
not even the joy of birdsong
can soothe their burning souls,
and their days are passed in silence
in the stillness of July heat.

But it is now they earn their colors;
it is now when they truly grow.
The tougher the road,
the stronger the soul—
the drink will taste sweeter than wine.

Borders

Nosing my boat against
the low muddy bank of the channel
marking the boundary of the refuge,
I can see the tell-tale hoof prints of deer
come down to the edge to drink.
In one spot off from the main area
deep depressions, slide marks show in the muck,
as if something had startled this young deer
bent over the water to quench her thirst.
Peering over the side of the boat, I see
against the bank a dug-out hollow
in the sandy bottom, a bream bed
where a mother bluegill had laid her eggs
to be fertilized, to start their arduous journey—
some to the gaping maws of bass or channel cat,
snapping turtle or needle-nosed gar,
others to grow larger, to develop the wanderlust
that will take them to a fate unknown
and perhaps eventually to a bed much like this.
The little deer must have been fascinated
with her reflection, peering into the mirrored surface,
soft, clouded sky and green branches above.
Surely she was entranced
when the water began to swirl and ripple like magic,
then suddenly explode with all the strength
of a mother protecting her nest:
eleven ounces of finned fury striking fear
in the heart of an eighty pound deer
that couldn't seem to dance away
quickly or gracefully enough,
and who would meekly seek out another venue
to sate her thirst,
to kiss the face
of these oh-so-mysterious waters.

Hurricane

"...a storm as big as Texas..."
the weatherman kept stating
over and over and we watched
as it two-stepped across the islands
twirling and swirling,
all barbed wire and tumbleweed,
scrub-brush and salt,
tipping its ten-million gallon hat
to young and old alike.
"...a storm as big as Texas..."
as if Texas herself had been torn
from the continental shelf
where she had rested all these years,
had been flung out to sea
and sent spinning like a top.

Inside this newly freed storm-state
a crinkle-faced grandma
in her red-checked apron
knuckle deep in biscuit dough
glances out
and shakes her head
at the sheets of rain
flapping over her clothesline,
worrying that her husband
is late coming home.

In the huge calm eye he swelters,
a weathered old fencepost of a man,
looking up at the still,
perfect blue of the Texas sky;
he leans on his hoe, pushes back
his State Fair straw hat
and prays that the rain'll hold off
'til he finishes just two more rows.
                              He knows
he must keep steady at it, must finish
before the great eye blinks shut
and all that he's worked for
is washed clean away
by what looks to be a real
rootin' tootin' sure-as-shootin' gully-washer.

End of Summer

For weeks now,
she had been teasing,
boiling cumulo-nimbus stew
there, on the horizon
above the river.
Sometimes, late in the afternoon,
we'd hear it—
the dry, hacking cough of thunder—
presaging a drawn-out display
of impotent heat lightning
in the clouds, so near, so far.
We waited and sweated,
we simmered as August
played the ham actor,
dying for days, for weeks,
until September poked
her nappy head above the horizon,
mischief and mayhem in her eyes.

Then, one evening,
it comes,
the low, rolling rumble
of a storm—
heavy with wet,
heady with cool,
and all is finally well
in our dust-choked, scorched,
withered and shriveled,
hard-tack crusted,
kiln-dried, sun-baked corner of heaven
as the first frog-fat drops
of Autumn
hop noisily
on a thirsty land,
on a people grateful
beyond any words.

Warclouds

Stark winds
blow storm clouds in—
battleships prepared for war

on their gray-green sides
dark bruises bloom
bring flashes of fire
rumble of guns

the battle is on

it will not end until
cold tears fill
ditch and hollow,
and roll like rivers
down the red clay hills
of home.

The Noah Gene

Don't be surprised
at the fear in the eyes
of your dog
as you walk him home
past the shipyards
just ahead of the storm.

Part Two: THE RAINS BEGIN

Life on the Surface

Beneath a slowly setting sun,
one by one,
pond turtles slide
off the jutting log—
    time-rounded teeth
    from an aging jawbone.

History of a Cloud

Once I was a cloud
floating lonely and high
the winds blew me
where they wished

In my great solitude
there was sadness
I would cover the sun
and cause misery
I would show up unannounced
and spoil plans

And I would cry
oh how I cried
when my tears fell
everyone ran for cover
everyone ducked inside
everyone
every one
but you

You stood outside
and cried with me
raised your face to mine
your tears were my tears
and mine yours

That is how
I fell to earth

Why I am no longer
a cloud.

Shooting Star

It was one of those nights when all was clear;
the cruel stars mocking me with icy stares,
jealously guarding the freedom of space.

I had taken to standing alone
outside at night, after dishes and kids and wife
had all been cleared from the kitchen.

Embracing the space between the stars, I stood hidden
in darkness, where no one could see the lines that worry
the corners of my eyes, or the gremlins
perched on my slumping shoulders, poking and prodding me to an early
end.

Lost in thought, I barely heard
the muffled thump of the screen door and the padded shooshing
of little feet on the grass. Suddenly there was warmth
as his small hand enclosed my fingers like a favorite glove.
Looking skyward, we watched in
silence.

I almost missed it as I gazed at his pale, upturned face—
a meteor streaked across the heavens in fiery splendor, and
I saw the light
reflected in his eyes, sparkling with a brilliance that rivaled the show
above.

        "Daddy, it sure goes by fast, doesn't it?"
        My breath caught in my throat, I replied, "Yes
        it does, son, way too fast."

We stood for a while hand in hand;
future and past connected by the touch of
now.

We searched with eyes and hearts and souls, still yearning,
but the stars had begun to blur.
Cold night air always did make my eyes water.

Daughter

I come to this lonesome place,
not often—
often enough to see
the coyote has been feeding well,
bits of bone and fur
among its droppings;
the rabbits and nervous field mice
yet flourish—
surgical hawks posted
like watchmen
atop the budding hickories and oaks;
the butterflies still
never fail to astonish—
matching the wildflower quilt
yellow for yellow, lavender for lavender,
fluttering like a sheen
over the field;
the buttery sunlight,
caught on the needles
of stiff-backed pines—
transformed into cascades
of golden jessamine,
its sweet scent
caressing me back,
                back,
                        the back of my hand floating
over the phone's luminous keypad—
hard plastic numbers
cold to the touch,
morphed into signals,
speeding along an unseen path,
clanging bells
summoning her voice
like ripples from the far side
of this darkening pond—
her voice lapping gently,
so near,
yet so very
long ago.

White Wedding

White—
blankpage white
like the snowflakes
that dance
swirling & curling
light as a father
in daughter's arms
whitegown swishes
the sound of wishes
piled high
as the drifts outside

He drifts outside
while his daughter twirls
in her husband's
loving arms
he turns
he sighs
he catches
her eye
in the light
of the cold clear pane

Love of his life
now someone's wife
his princess
floating away
one perfect flake
hits his outstretched hand—
how quickly it melts
away.

Bird

You had to be careful, let go just right,
rough, scaly skin of the vine worn smooth
by countless leaps of faith — was it 10, 15, 20
feet up in that gnarled old friend of a tree?
Hands spit-shined for palm-slick freedom,
that one brief moment when earth's heavy fingers let loose,
when you could almost feel feathers growing,
then down, down, back down to the grip and the pull,
the ground like a lap in a pine-straw skirt
as you fell in a muffled rush, smile glued on by the wind,
then jumped to your feet and scrambled back up,
battered, not beaten, to grab
    just one more piece of the wind,
    to fly like a bird once again.

Only a Boy

We are squatting at the edge
of a stand of oak and hickory,
early morning sunlight splattering
like napalm on the leaf-bed.
My son, nearly invisible
in camouflage, shotgun resting
in his lap, cranes his neck
to scan the treetops: eyes searching
for the least skitter of movement,
fur on branch; ears attuned
to crack of acorn, thump
of falling shell.
His youngboy face is serious,
intense, anticipating the dash
of squirrel from flash
of the gunbarrel, and I am

> once again on the tarmac, watching,
> as the cavernous plane rumbles earthward,
> jungle steam trailing from its wings
> in the gray of November, in a cold steel rain.
> Stern-eyed men in camouflage
> unload boxes draped in flags,
> inappropriate presents at a
> homecoming party from Hell.
> He was only a boy, only a boy
> squatting beneath the trees,
> craning his neck and watching
> for slightest movement, listening
> for lightest rustle above,
> and acorns of fire rained down,
> limb from limb torn asunder,
> rain and thunder, only a boy.

Continued

A muffled explosion, and I'm back,
watching the squirrel tuck and fall,
land with a thud and lie still.
I run to my son and hug him, and
I hold him just a little tighter,
squeeze him just a little longer,
his body engulfed in my arms,
his smile etched on my heart.

Diamonds, Rubies

Silhouetted in the headlights
of her idling car
she could be coming home
from work
from shopping
home to loving arms
to welcoming smile
a kiss
through the rain-pocked glass
she could be an angel
floating in a sea
of diamonds

Scanning the suddenly larger
colder room
breath catches
just once
eyes blink back tears
picture clears

Muffled clank
of metal on metal
outside
she slams the door
on a dream
her tail lights burn
like rubies
brief flares
grow smaller
more distant
their warm red glow
a burning deceit—
the reality
hard as cold stone.

The Old McLemore Place

I can feel, more than see, their presence
in the shadows beneath these old oaks;
their whispers the breeze that stirs in the trees,
rising like cookfire smoke.

The house has been gone for years now,
the fencewire rusted with time;
the occasional post, a weathered old ghost,
lies covered in bramble and vine.

But here is the path to their garden,
where their sweat salted many a meal;
where the tooth of the plow turned what is now
a carapace, a crust, and a seal.

And here is the path to the creek-bed
which flowed free and clear in its time;
the Spring and the Fall brought water for all,
the Summer and Winter were dry.

The last man to live here is gone now,
few even remember his face;
and yet, to this day, the locals still say
"Oh, that's the old McLemore Place."

Sense of Place and Order

The old order changeth, yielding place to new...
Tennyson
The Passing of Arthur

The place where my father worked smelled
of lemon oil rubbed deep in burnished wood;
of fresh-cut gladiola, lily and iris.
It held tight the scents of old women's powder
and dime store cologne,
of Saturday night soap
on a week's worth of kid.

Saturday mornings, I'd meet him there,
his fingers purpled with mimeograph ink,
and we'd feed the blank bulletins
through the hand-cranked printer
to roll out stamped and ordered, a program,
the methodical shoop-chukka-shoop
a weekly reminder that the big picture remains,
only the details change.

The walls of my father's workplace resounded
with the lilt of old songs,
of untrained voices cured by smoke
or grated shrill from the agonies
of lives lived raw and hard;
voices spent calling cows to barns
and children to supper,
arguing bills and yessirring bosses
in a struggle without end (amen, amen).

The soft, hallowed air in his workplace
was flecked with motes of dust,
refugees from countless swipes
of rag, of cloth and dry-mop,
tiny angels dancing just out of reach
of the grasp of a curious child.

Continued

Once, twice, three times a week,
my father threw open the doors
and beckoned all who would to come in,
sit for a while and listen, sing and reflect,
and make sense of this place called home.

I still drive by on occasion—
it's changed, as have we all—
the steeple's gone, it seems smaller;
but even now sometimes I smell
a faint tang of lemon and flowers,
hear a shoop-chukka-shoop
in the purple night air,
sense order on pages
grown blank with time.

The Beaver

His house has fallen into disrepair,
its once-proud dome which perched
like a hardhat on the headwaters
he himself had dammed.
With slick clay mud
he'd bound the sticks,
stacked and set them strong and sure
to keep him warm and dry and safe
in this sparkling, liquid world.

While he yet lived, no stick was lost,
no wall was breached, no leak was brooked;
with sturdy muscle, stoutest will,
he'd patched, repaired, replaced, and shored
the weak spots in his fortress home.

But now he's gone,
and left behind,
a sad, abandoned shell now sits;
the weeds and rushes have sprouted there,
and in the summer evening breeze,
the rooster grasses bob and weave—
    defiant plumes on a battered bonnet
    in the street after Easter's parade.

Instructions for the Design of a Kimono

To begin, the fabric should be fluid,
moving without its wearer;
it must speak in shadow-whispers,
like the needles of the pines.
Its color should be deep and rich,
the gloaming green
of a loblolly thicket
in the ghostlight after a rain.
It must invite the touch
as the pines themselves
beckon and coo
to the lucky who find their shade.

The egrets should be sewn
of snow-white thread;
they must ride the grey limbs of the cypress
like whitecaps on the sea,
feathers ruffled in evening breeze,
dark eyes closed, beaks safely sheathed
in the folds of their limber necks.
The pool below should dance
with a seething shimmer of fish—
the glint of gleaming silver
reflecting in the still, black eye
of the wader on the shoreline,
a solemn, strutting samurai,
orange sword drawn and poised
for this dance beneath the moon.

The Fishwife's Tale

She had seen it sparkling
in the sunlight at her feet
in the busy market;
she knew before she stooped
to pick it up
what it was,
what it meant,
and the wave of memories
that would come crashing home
when she touched it...

All those long years together,
mending and tending the nets,
scraping barnacles and crust
from the bow,
oiling slickers and boots,
and enduring the smell!
Oh, the heavy, brine tang
of the ocean,
of fish by the ton,
year after year washing by,
condensed like a droplet now to this—
one shining fish scale
     plucked from the street,
weighing her life in the balance.

Through all those years,
pulled by the tides,
sweet moments purchased
with the salt of the deep,
the salt of their sweat,
her one constant dream
had been this:
to retire to a dry place,
the air soft with flowers,
where winds don't whip up a froth;

Continued

where the songs of the night
aren't driven
by the lap-lap-lap of the waves;
a place dry and warm and far from
the cold, sharp lure of the sea.

At sunset now, in her porch swing,
she rolls back and forth in the breeze,
searching the western horizon
for his boat to come in from the sea.

Part Three: DELUGE

Life Oak

The huge live oak had stood for a hundred years
in front of our little house hard by the coast.
She looked to be leaning, forever leaning
out toward the street, as if searching
up and down, waiting for her people to return home.
When the city first built sidewalks in the late 40's,
they had wanted to remove the tree;
Grandpa said, "No. The tree stays."
So they constructed their walk
with a little zig, a little zag around the twisted oak.
For years, she stood her ground leaning and watching
as my folks moved back home after Grandpa died.
She watched out for me, for my brothers, my sisters
as we grew, then flew and scattered,
as we returned again and again and again.
There were storms, God yes—
Betsy, Camille, and countless others,
but still the old oak stood watch
over our little fortress against the sea.
Then came a roiling, boiling, blowhard
water-witch of a storm named Katrina,
spitting wind and water and raw fury
tossing tons of people's lives and livelihoods
like so much flotsam, like useless trinkets
to be toyed with then abandoned, scattered in ruin.
I don't know which caught her first—
the great, hulking shrimp boat
or our neighbor's Buick wagon,
but both ended up hitting the leaning tree,
one high, one low, like a picture-perfect tackle,
and, old roots loosened by the flood,
bones brittle from age, she let go—
toppling back, back, back and over
onto our little house,
a sprawling exclamation point
to our screamed surrender.

Continued

Her watch is over now; she's no longer needed
to keep the faith, to will us home,
a home that is only a memory now, an empty lot,
a curious detour around a gaping hole
on a sidewalk leading to nowhere.

Wash & Dry

The preacher loosed his words
(like a flood);
I must have ducked—
I'm dry as a bone.

Still Waters

Like fog and mist
I am water
like cloud and sea
I am water
I am the waters of those before me
and the waters of those around me
they course through my veins as rivers
the waters swirl and rise
they swell and flow
as dreams in the night
as stories told, songs sung
I am water
and water begets water
and water's water
without end
and all I can do
is roll with the waves
add my pinch of salt
and be gone in the wash
like fog and mist
gathering again
like cloud and sea...

You are water...

Blue Boy

In the pulsing blue of squad-car lights
divers emerge from the half-frozen pond
pulling him from water's icy grip;
kicking and screaming, his mother breaks
from the arms of neighbors,
of friends, of those who knew
this beautiful boy, now
blue-skinned and stiff,
laid out on the bank—
beautiful in death,
tragic and still
dripping in the wet air, sloughing
what had rushed into his lungs—
chest bared and pounded,
cold blue lips receiving
the hot-hopeful breaths of life,
mother frantic, fists full of hair,
muffling her wails on the breast
of a stranger,
a stranger who knows
that this precious son,
this beautiful blue-skinned boy
is gone,
and in words that slip out
cold and unbidden as ice,
he comfortably lies,
"It's all right now,
it'll be all right."

Final Fling

On a sandbar
at a bend in the river
I watched the dead
play volleyball
pale limbs akimbo
as they leapt & spiked
blocked & dug
They were tireless
their laughter was hollow
barking off
the gray sand
the murky water
of a sluggish summer current

Later
around a blazing bonfire
I watched the dead
roast wieners
wolf their toasted marshmallows
deathwake over flickering flames
I watched & listened
as they spoke last goodbyes
grabbed last hugs
kissed cheeks whose warmth
they'd never feel again

Next morning
a red-eyed sun rose heavily
phones rang
voices cracked
tears appeared
like phantoms

Who could have known
on a turnpike out of Chicago
at a toll booth in the outside lane
they'd be scattered
like so much loose change

Who knew our goodbyes were for good
          our farewells so very unfair.

Crossing Over

The old opossum teeters
across the gravel, narrow
jaws grappling with
an unseen foe, dark
eyes already beginning
to resemble the X's you see
on the cartoon dead.
He has left behind his world,
a kingdom of vine
and canopy,
a larder filled
with wild grape and persimmon,
with fat, juicy grubs and
things dead—
oh, how he loved
those special found treats,
ripening on forest floor,
calling to insect pilgrims
like a shrine
stinking to high heavens.

Now, here in the fading sunlight,
on this little-used logging road,
he comes to die,
to lie at the edge
and calibrate his heartbeat
to the drum of Mother Earth.
His breathing labors,
he trembles.
His heart beats slow...
then slower...
as the shadow of a
circling vulture grows larger,
as the dying breeze
ruffs his fine grey coat,
as the pilgrims line up
to march.

Wake-up

I had always heard it
flashed before your eyes,
this cell-thin act called
Life.

I started
awake in closed-throat panic unable to breathe to speak to view
the docudramedy in which, for forty plus years,
I had starred in recurring role.
Instead, I could only shake
her awake and answer sleep-muffled query
with shallow gasps and eyes dilated in
fear.
Stumbling to bathroom,
gasping and grasping the sink,
leaning and cupping my hand to drink,
unable to swallow, I noticed
    a glob of nearly dried toothpaste,
    a day-glo blue
    jellyfish (with added whiteners!),
    washed ashore on the porcelain sea;
    the small pail of hairbrushes clogged
    with strands of family DNA;
    the hamper which lolls with a mouthful of clothes,
    socks hanging out like tongues.
Each passing second takes minutes;
each heartbeat pounds quicker than that;
calmly methodical wife tries to keep life
flowing in and out of my lungs.
I realize I've spoken my last
Iloveyou
and, desperately I sign.
She takes it to mean my heart has quit beating,
and rushes to steady my fall.

Continued

I nibble small bites of sweet, sterile air,
as ambulance doors swing
shut.
A long, lonely wail and flashes of light roll
down the road in the night.

I'd always heard that it flashes
before you
go.

Faith of My Father

It was nothing you'd see draped
on a hanger in his closet;
it was nothing sealed in plastic
from the cleaners down the street.
It was nothing handed down
from religious hierarchy,
an icon steeped in history
and meant to be locked away.

He didn't have to polish it
when company was coming;
it never had to hang outside
to air out or to dry.
It was nothing he could tear or muss,
or stain or ever lose;
it was invisible, it was visible
in everything he did.

And, when at last, he faced the end,
on linens white as snow,
the background hum of instruments
strumming peacefully as harps,
flourescence beaming down on him
was met with an inner glow.
He filled his lungs and straightened out,
then slipped into the pool,

> a lone and graceful swimmer
> backstroking through the waves,
> smiling with anticipation for
> those waiting on the other shore.

Buffaloes

When I am old, I shall go out West
to see what's left of the Plains;
no more will I roam
from the buffalo's home
while the breath in these lungs remains.

And there, on a rock or the rise of a hill,
I'll watch the behemoths graze
on grass that was born
next to Indian corn
in bygone and whygone days.

After a while, if I gain their trust,
perhaps an old one will come;
we'll study each other,
a kinship of brothers,
in tune with the beat of our drums.

Though I can't know what a buffalo knows,
and he cannot know my mind,
proudly we'll stand
in this wind-swept land,
separate, but two of a kind.

He shouldered the weight of a nation
in its rush to the Western shore;
the everyday strife
of a comfortable life
was the heaviest burden I bore.

And when we've turned to prairie dust,
the world may not miss the sound
of a poet whose words,
like the buffalo herds,
no longer raise clouds as they pound,

At the Bird Museum

I catch myself
whistling softly
along with their
eerie recordings—
   disembodied songs
   taking flight
   in dead air.

The Theory of Devolution

Salt-spray flecks his face,
warm waves beckon.
Overhead, gulls wheel and cry.
Stepping into the brine,
he looks down:
feet slowly devolve
as sand and sea
cover toes,
leave flipper-like
appendages,
smooth and streamlined,
built for swimming,
built for diving,
for feeding on the power
of the sea.
He steps further,
then further still.
Legs merge and meld,
pale skin morphs to gray-blue,
hands dangle useless beneath the water,
flatten to form fins.

He submerges,
breathing
the salty oxygen
bubbling below,
gills work harder,
eyes grow membranes,
lips firm, scales weigh in.
He surfaces one last time,
glances behind,
sees strange footprints
trickling
down
 the
beach,
wonders just whose
they were.

nor these symbols of Western freedom:
for hundreds of years they ranged,
writing their story
in thunder and glory,
then, far too quickly, things changed.

Let my words collect dust on a bookshelf;
let the bison herds freeze in their frames;
our Spirits shall fly
in that pioneer sky
while a prairie wind calls out our names.

      And our wandering dust shall settle
      to rest on the wide-open Plains;
      contented, we'll sigh as we lie there
      'til our memory is all that remains.

Vespers

In the little park
down the street
laughter,
like small prayers,
rises one celebration at a time.
Amid fresh scrapes of soil
and chalked lines
knuckles are tightened,
lips are pursed and bitten.
Here, a false sun glistens
on the cheek-trickle of tears
as we sit stiffly
shoulder to shoulder
alone
by fresh scrapes,
dirt piled and covered
with unnatural carpet,
death feeding on life
feeding death.
In the forever distance children
giggle, children
scream, children
play, children
grow (all too quickly),
old.

Part Four: RAINBOW

After the Storm

stray crimson leaf
from neighbor's tree—
    bright Oz moment
in the gray Kansas at my feet.

Coastal Warfare

The marsh periwinkle snail thrives
in these coastal backwaters
when others might turn away;
it marches inexorably, slowly,
an appetite on the half-shell
as the wetlands die—
   dry winds and drought
   sap the strength
   of the rough-edged grasses,
their whispered rustle and rasp
both death knell
and dinner bell
for these insatiable
voracious warriors,
trails of slime
marking the time
of the grasses'
inevitable doom.

After the Rain

There's a place in the woods I sometimes go
to wander when feeling alone.
After the rain, in this clearcut field,
I'll sift through the dirt and the stone.

And scattered across that hidden place
lie the remnants of times gone by:
arrowheads chipped from ancient stone
jut out, as if ready to fly,

ready to sink their sharpened tips
into flesh unprepared for the pain.
I pick them up gently and carry them home
to study them, after the rain.

There's a place in my heart I sometimes go
when life makes me feel alone.
And after the tears have fallen like rain,
I'll wander this place that's grown

rigid and cold, with pieces of dreams
that were shattered and left to die,
jagged-edged memories that cut like knives,
and loves that have passed me by,

sharp words that stuck in yielding flesh
inflicting a deep-seated pain.
I'll cover them up and bury them deep,
and forget them, until the next rain.

Today

Behind me,
as far back as I can see,
my footprints,
splayed and pressed
in the fresh morning dew
which never seems to evaporate,
but instead, like a shimmer
balanced on the pinprick
of the sun,
holds in its dampened grip
all that I've been
and nods at the place
where even now I'm poised
to take the next step,
to leave the spot from which
only moments ago
I would have bet my life
I'd not be moved—
not by the wildest of horses
nor the unbridled pull
of the moon.

Advice

Every storm is different;
every storm the same.
Pressure builds, pressure falls.
In the distance sometimes
are rumblings—
ominous and low.
Learn to read them.
Take shelter, duck,
prepare for the worst;
sometimes they pass,
but they'll return.
It is wise always to be vigilant;
not all storms give warning,
not all storms give time.
Some come at night
(from nothing)—
suddenly boiling and breaking,
striking and striking and...

You must never feed the storms
your fear.
Instead, set your mouth
in a hard line;
gradually dare to curl
a smile.
Each storm you face is different;
every storm the same.

Outsiders

Turn around and
we are foreigners
aliens in an instant
   (the wording of a letter,
     low voices on the phone).
In a flash we can be
plucked from our beds
snapped free
like the old hickory
propped on one gnarled elbow
wondering at
its jagged fray of a trunk
shattered like old bone
in the night wind.

A blink of the eye
the wag of a tail
a poke and a prod
and we're gone
whisked away.

Now here alone
among native and homesteader
namesakes whose histories
are branded
on streets
on walls
on trees
on land
fresh from the unfamiliar
   (sore thumb,
     costumed stranger)
lone grains of sand
introduced but unknown
irritants hoping
some day and some way
to become
as pearls.

Roots

The strain had been established
long before their seeds had landed
on the sea-beaten Carolina shores.
Even then, there was purpose to their path,
hooking south from English moors,
        south from Scottish hills,
fleeing English tyrant,
        Scottish want.

These seeds took hold
in mountain soil—
firm rock and forest loam—
then slowly, ever steadily,
spread out on gentle breeze,
to settle in the wildlands
across the Mississippi,
sinking tap roots in the sands,
pressing red clay's hands
in a hardy grip that said
at last,
"I'm home."

Song

First light
lying in bed listening
coveting the birds
their dreamless sleep
their joyous awakenings
all twitter and fluff
bright song in their hearts
light sonnet set free
on the morning air
then off to work
to the inexorable dance and drudge
of hunger and thirst
of hunter and hunt
some thing to do
all the long day
one thing bleeds
into another
beating the air incessantly
with their wings
though in the end
the air wins.
It always wins
and they return to rest the night
long lonely night
'til morning comes
and with it the song
ever the song.

My song differs
in form in fashion
the groans and grunts
of bedded stiffness
the mumbling stumble
to coffee pot
to kitchen window
outside which a pair
of yellow-throated vireos
perch in the redbud
offering me their
heart-felt song
before whistling away
to work.

October, Country

It usually starts
as the Summer dog days
are digging their holes.
August spreads
her heavy fingers
just enough to reveal
a glimpse of September;
    a crackle in the air,
        blush of crimson on black gum leaf,
        whiff of North-country breeze,
        acorns ripening in the oaks.

At night, sometimes, I'll hear her
rummaging through her pouch,
(practice points, broadheads,
grunt call, knife), taking inventory
of hunts to come,
when October flings open her door.

She tells me she needs hay,
four bales, stacked neatly
in the yard. She stretches
her arms; sinews strain
as she draws the tensioned bow-string.
Her pinpoint aim
camouflages the flame
of orange and gold
in her eyes.
The arrow flies
and softly burrows to the heart
of this grassy deer—boundless,
and bound with twine.

She smiles
as Autumn paints a blush
on her cheeks.

Crow's Feet

Forever defined
in terms of straight lines,
these birds of impeccable taste
in shiny black suits,
with stiff-legged gait
strut to their roadside fare.

I used to love
to honk at them,
to make them spread their wings,
or better, to bend their
stiffened knees, preparing
for sudden flight.

Then,
when I'd passed,
they returned—
stiff and straight as ever,
feathers unruffled and eyes
on their prize again.

I watch you at breakfast
as morning lights
your eyes, and coffee steams
a thousand questions
in the air
between our hearts.

I don't see them
tracking from your eyes
like the ones I can't ignore
in the mirror, marking the edges
of laughter, the miles of smiles
I've traveled holding your hand.

Continued

Haven't I given you pleasure enough,
and joy to crease your eyes?
The beauty of curve on curve on
softly falling slope needs
the lines, straight lines
to mark,
to startle and enhance.

Now, as you cradle your cup and gently blow
a breathy foreplay to a caffeine kiss,
    I get the urge to honk
        and make you bend in laughter;
        I want to see the crow's feet
        and know
        we're still in love.

Toy Soldiers, Hardwood Floor, Bag of Marbles, and Two Small Boys

With a snap
and a rustle of plastic,
both the seal and
the truce
are broken;
soldiers tumble
to hardwood—
dark green us,
desert-tan them,
best two out of three,
then switch sides.

Each plastic warrior prays
as he's placed in a neat little row
to present such a narrow target
he'll be missed by
the roll of the death-ball,
escape the crushing blow.

Good soldiers all,
they face it head-on,
until the bitter end—
battered and bruised,
defeated again
by the uncanny persistence
and accurate arms
of these little gods,
hurling spheres of glass
at soldiers whose daily views
are deja-vu's
of death, death by rolling thunder—
then they're packed and shoved back under
the beds of these rambunctious gods,
these generals
in footie pajamas
who sleep the sleep of sweet victory,
who dream of wars
to come.

EPILOGUE

Postscript to the Epistle to the Animals Who Missed the Ark

It wasn't your fault
by any means
no
it was it always was
and still is
our blame to bear
not that it helps you now
but know these things:
your kind persists
thriving in corners
in pockets of paradise
valiant in defense
against extinction
your remnant has adapted
taken the hand
it was dealt
and played for all
it was and is
and will ever be worth

How ironic that
when everything is said and done
we really are all
in the same boat

About the Author

Jim Barton is a poet and storyteller from the Ouachita River bottomlands in south Arkansas . He has had work published in such journals as *Mississippi Review, Louisiana Literature, The Lyric, Timber Creek Review, The Mid-America Poetry Review* and others. He has performed his work on stage, on college campuses and radio. His writings in poetry, fiction and nonfiction have won many awards, most recently the Sybil Nash Abrams Award and a Jim Stone Grand Prize. Jim is the 2008 winner of the John and Miriam Morris Chapbook Contest. He is a member of Poets' Roundtable of Arkansas, National Federation of State Poetry Societies, the Poetry Society of Virginia and two area writers' groups. He gathers inspiration from the natural world, which never ceases to amaze him.